unstable
as water

unstable as water

a collection of poetry

V. Renée Cutting

To order additional copies of this book, contact:
Xlibris Corporation
1-888-795-4274
www.Xlibris.com
Orders@Xlibris.com
25115

CONTENTS

My mother, Valma Rose Marie, you gave me the talents of my great-grandmother, Millicent Best; the beauty of my grandmother Lolita Walker; and the blessings of your unconditional love. Thanks for teaching me the joy of sharing these gifts.

FOREWORD

Unstable As Water
(Genesis 49:4 KJV)

As a child growing up on the tiny island of Barbados, I had the ability to walk through the Atlantic Ocean to anywhere in the universe simply by sitting on the beach and reading a book.

At the impressionable age of twelve, I actually took flight across the ocean, only to discover that life on the other side of my mind's eye was not what I had imagined it would be. My only true memory of that day of departure was how much I wondered why I couldn't live amongst the mountains of clouds. I was dismayed by how quickly the pallid billows had replaced the tie-dyed blue and white waves of the ocean and descended to bury the shelled little girl beneath the corals of the sand.

I began writing my first collection of poetry, *Unstable As Water*, by casting the first line out as a buoy to rescue the image of that little girl, frolicking around in a frog green bikini swimsuit with sparkles of ecru sand splintered between a few strands of hair and dreaming about life on the other side. This collection chronicles my journey through many unstable waters, which have all led my spirit to rediscover that there are limitless possibilities for transformation.

Each day as I walk through this universe, I unearth more of a stable path simply by sitting still in myself and reading and writing the book of my life.

ACKNOWLEDGMENT

Thank you mother for your whole-hearted support, words of wisdom and for just always being there.

Daddy, your zest for life is an inspiration. Thanks for letting me know I was born a stargirl.

My sister, Vicki, and my brother, Mark, I love you for being my biggest fans, but simply for just being you.

Donnette, Norvella, Trixie, and my Uncle Bruce, thank you for editing my words and emotions.

Judy Renacia, thank you for capturing the essence of my words in your brilliant cover design.

My family, friends, and all my supporters, I am extremely grateful for your endless encouragement.

ICE-CUBED SCULPTURES

STARGIRL

I felt
Ordinary
Nondescript
A predictable miracle
Just rising
And falling
With the sun
For I never knew
The sun
Was a star.

SECRETS OF THE HEART

Inspired by 2 Corinthians 4:7-9

My heart has been searching
To find the woman I used to be.
When I first stood and watched
The universe's birth,
I made the time
To watch time be born.

Before matter mattered
And space had no space,
I was made
And summoned by my name
To be a
Woman.

But sometime between the creation
Of time and infinity,
When chaos gave way to the cosmos,
I lost myself in the deep red seas
That flowed down my thighs.
I have been swimming in the disguise
Of who I used to be.

My heart has been searching
To find my secret treasure
Buried right here in this jar of clay.
Beneath the spherical depths
Of the earth's stratosphere and troposphere
I've been lost
In this atmospheric pressure of life,
But I am still standing up!

Standing in my daughter's blood
Crying out from the dust of the world.
She was shot down and killed
In a school library
Because she had the audacity to say,
Yes I believe in Jesus.
Now come on, what is the matter with us?

What is the matter with me, they ask,
Allowing myself to be beaten down like a drum
And signing up for the club of
Battered-women syndrome?
In pain,
I'm battered,
My life is shattered,
And although it does not seem to matter,
I am still standing up!

Standing in detonating land mines
East of Cambodia
With amputated legs,
I am still standing up!

Standing high up in a tree in Mozambique
With the roof of my house
Floating in the great floods below me.
With contractions and hunger
I gave birth to a child,
Born in a tree.
Now that is the power of some
Unknown known Spirit
Growling inside of me.

For I have found power in hunger
And when everything is out of control
Outside of me,
I am in total control of what I place inside of me.
Kissing the ground from fainting and starving,
Sometimes I can't stand to look at me.
But despite that
I can't control the fact
That I am still standing up!

Rising on a pot of chicken soup steam
For its scent is the remnant of my mother
Who was eaten alive
By a cancerous tumor
And then died.
Her screams scratch pains in my eyes,
I cry
And I hate that age-old
Unanswerable question
Why?

I am lonely.
I am tired.
I am worried.
I am burdened.
But I am still standing up!

My husband has left the three kids and me
For another guy.
The baby is crying, and my bosom's milk
Has dried up and has curdled,
And tomorrow is greeting me with
A good morning and another hurdle,
To get over the man of my dreams
Who in reality was only just a dream.
But in order for me to keep it real,
My reality has to be real.
Really.

Sometimes the secrets of our hearts
Are buried deep down in imaginary places,
Where the faces of our times
Hibernate in what is seen
Instead of dancing
With the unseen beating of the heart.
That is why I do not lose heart,
Because I cannot lose heart
And bury myself within
The secrets of my heart.
Though outwardly I am wasting away,
Inwardly I am being renewed day by day,
By the beating of my heart
Which takes a mere six liters of blood
And runs twelve thousand laps
Through the highways of my veins,
In just one given day.
Now you know that is the only way
That I am still standing up!

Standing amidst the darkness,
Sometimes I fail to see
That there are zillions of bright lights
Beaming inside of me.
I've got trillions of cells
Dancing up and down my spine.
I've got trillions of cells
Promenading up and down my spine.
I've got trillions of cells that you don't even see
Do-si-doing up and down my spine
Because quite simply
I am profoundly,
Fearfully
And wonderfully made
With prolific double-helix strands of DNA pearls
That wrap themselves around themselves
And make love to themselves,
So that I can define myself
And know myself
And love myself
And simply be myself
Because there is only one self
That I am,
A treasure in a jar of clay.
I am being pulled on and molded,
Sculpted and hardened,
And if broken,
I still remain standing up!

Standing holding the creation of mankind
In the center
Of my womb which has given birth
To great leaders,
Murderers,
All the unsung heroes,
And the cries of every child's voice.
Now that is the freedom of choice,
For I have been chosen amongst
Emeralds and rubies and sapphires
To be the true treasure of this universe.
My offspring gave birth to the diamond,
The Rock that you have been looking for,
The Rock that you have been hoping for,
The Rock that you have been praying for,
The Rock of the foundation
On which I am standing.
Because
I'm Still Standing Up!
Because somebody has got to have my back!
"When I am hard pressed on every side but not crushed,
Perplexed but not in despair,
Persecuted but not abandoned,
Struck down but not destroyed."
Someway,
Somehow,
I still remain standing up!
Because I keep getting that little pat on the back
The one that lets you know you are all of that—
Which is nothing
But just a microscopic mist,
Like a speck of dust.

So, Daughters of the Dust,
Rise up!
Stand up!
So when the creator of the universe
Summons you by name,
You better know who you are
At the end of the day
And stand when he says,
Come out of the tomb
Of the womb of this world and
Dance!

BRING IT ON!

"Love is patient,
Love is kind.
It does not envy,
It does not boast,
It is not proud.
It is not rude,
It is not self-seeking,
It is not easily angered,
It keeps no record of wrongs.
Love does not delight in evil
But rejoices with the truth.
It always protects,
Always trusts,
Always hopes,
Always perseveres.
Love never fails . . .
Now we see but a poor reflection as in a mirror;
then we shall see face to face.
Now I know in part; then I shall know fully,
even as I am fully known."
1 Corinthians 13

I looked into the mirror,
And I saw a reflection
A reflection of a child—
A special child—
Me!

From the reflection there came a light,
One side was shining brightly
And the other was obscure.

Have you ever been in love with yourself?
The face you see in the mirror—
The reflection
That only reflects who you are?

Falling in love with the dichotomized self
Is an intimate love affair.
Living and learning to love the dark phases
Often leaves one to lose sight of the bright stages.

When the spirit of darkness
Veils itself in pain—
The kind of pain
That makes you roll around
On the ground,
Like a serpent
Tempting you with trepid temptations,
Leaving you in stages of pure frustration—
It is then I say,
Bring it on!
Bring it on!
I love you
Because my love is patient,
My love is kind—
The kind of love
That does not envy your power over me.
So bring it on!
Bring it on!

I can bear it
I can handle it
I can stand up under it.

This is not a battle of boasting.
I acknowledge your aphrodisiac power
When you have lulled me
Into a deep, weak sleep.
But when I wake up
And I am impregnated
With an unaborted spirit
Of divine power,
It is then I say,
Bring it on!
Bring it on!

This love-hate relationship
Does not make me proud or rude.
I do not seek pleasure
From satisfying your personal desires.
I'm not easily angered by your goal
Of constantly aiming to purchase my full soul.

Yet at the same time,
The hardest part about loving you
Is how hard it is to discard
All the rights and the wrongs
Because when I hear the voice—
The voice of that child in the mirror
Crying out in the night—
It is hard to love.
It is hard to forgive.
It is hard not to give in and delight in evil
Instead of rejoicing in the truth—
Because your love for distorting the truth
Makes it hard to see
That the evilness is true
But it is not the Truth—
Because
The Truth protects.
The Truth trusts.

The Truth hopes.
The Truth perseveres.
So when I cry out in the night
And say
Bring it on!
Bring it on!
Bring it on!
The Truth will never fail me.

When I look into the mirror
And I see the reflection—
The reflection of a poor child
Crying out in the night—
When it stands face to face with the light,
Face to face I see
That even in the darkest moments of the night,
There are hundreds of bright stars
Piercing through the dark sky,
And even quarter moons
Are never overpowered
By the tower of the night.

Face to face
I have to face and look at myself
I reflect on myself,
My dichotomized self,
My imperfect self
Disappearing.
I have to face
And look within myself
To see my perfect self
Reappearing.
I fall in love with myself.
I fall in love with the complete woman that I am.
I fall in love with the special woman that I am.
I fall in love with the *I am* in me!

FULFILLMENT

I am so full of my
Self
Made to doubt what I am
About
Face I turn to face who I am
Becoming
Still at attention to the details of my
Senses
Which sense the threats of internal civil wars
Under
Attack, I am beginning to understand I can stand
Under
Garments and be in
Full
Bloom in size-A cups overflowing with
Bounty
Hunters who hunt for my head
Full
Of cornrows sectioned off in
Part
I am fully known in
Circles
Which have become lines to
Divide
And section off the worlds I
Grew
Up in small places in big
Spaces
Filled with voids and
Avoidances
To the sound of

Silence
That breeds in the underground tenants of my
Soul
Holds onto the fleeting moments of
Self
Fulfillment and its implication that my formless
Being
Is to be filled with the
Peace
That transcends all understanding, so I can stand
Under
My selfless self and
Be
Fulfilled.

LIQUID DREAMS

VIRGIN LIMBO

I. Bonds

Sometimes
Dreams are buried
At the bottom of the ocean,
Weighed down by a
Tiny strand of sand that bonds with another—
Tiny strand of sand that bonds with another—
Tiny strand of sand that bonds our dreams in bondage,
Yet the water flows—
And so we go with the flow
We don't know we are flowing in.
Current—times—tide—all—waved—off
From being rescued
From each other
And ourselves.
Washed ashore,
Unsure
Of who we are—
The daughters of our mothers
And our grandmothers
Who laid our bodies down
And stretched our legs wide,
Circumcised
In unsterilized societal cycles
We are
Washed out,
Wrung out,
Hung out
To dry—
With hands outstretched and

Closed-pinned
To the sky
We look for answers to the question
Why?

II. Our Mothers Always Said: "Once Mad, Always Mad!"

Why?—Z!
Is what our mothers always said:
And now that you know your ABCs,
Next time won't you play with me?
So we play with the *ABCs* of life
And respond to unanswered letters
To write the stories of our lives.
As we search for the meanings
Beneath the lines,
We often go too far out and
Too deep for our reality
Until we remember what our mothers always said:
You better not go too far out there
Because the sea does not have a backdoor.
Therefore then
We stay ashore,
Unsure
Of who we are,
And we go with the flow
We don't know we are flowing in—
But what we do know is
There has to be
Something in the water
Because of course
That is what our mothers always said—
Something sexual and mystical,
Unavoidably responsible
For this madness
Between you and I.
So please forgive the madness
But that is who we are—

Virgins in limbo.
With our backs to the ground,
We are going under
But forever looking upward
To the sky
For answers to the question
Why?

III. On the Other Side of the Pole

Like why are we constantly
Lying in waiting,
Wondering
When this world will come to an end.
Before we wrap our legs
Around the clouds,
Cry,
And squeeze out the living waters—
For in the waters
Are the recycled
Years of tears—
Plagued with the fears
Of our mothers and our grandmothers,
Who laid our bodies down
And stretched our legs wide
Straight across the equator line
And up and down
The North Pole and the South Pole,
With the hopes that
We would be in search
Of their lost souls—
Lost in the flow
That we don't even know we are flowing in.
But we are here and they are there
Somewhere on the other side—
Somewhere on the other side
Were all these women who
Ran to the edge of the world

Only to find out what they were running from
Was still waiting there—
At the back of our world
When it tilts on its axis,
They were left there—
Women on the edge,
Who stood in watch
As their worlds peeled back
From the edges of the waters.
They looked on—
As the continents drifted.
They held on—
As the waters parted.
They walked on—
The water they didn't even know
We would now be flowing in.
Because we are here and they are there
Somewhere on the other side—
Somewhere on the other side
Was that little girl running
Without running water—
Who ran in search
Of some form of living water.
Before she reached puberty
She ran past her identity—
Her uncoiled fingerprints
Were ripped to shreds
Like threads
Of silkworms
Steeped in scalded waters
And sewn in between
The unseen seams
Of the clothes
That we now proudly wear.
But we are here and she is there
Somewhere on the other side—
Somewhere on the other side
Was the woman

Whose blood was run to water—
Broken.
Like fragmented
Fibroids of cotton fields,
Our survival was her only shield
Against this world
Which denied her
The right to be right here.
But we are here and she is there
Somewhere on the other side—
Somewhere on the other side
Was a woman at pause.
After a life of running
From her change of life,
She arose
Out of the streams of her conscience
And removed her veil,
Only to be beheaded
And finally opened enough to say:
I just want to be heard
I just want to be heard
Can you hear me?
Can you hear me?
But we are here and she is there
Somewhere on the other side.
But why, Mother—
Why?

IV. Unstable Waters

Why are we here and they are there?
All these women who gathered
Their clothes and went down
To the well—
To be well—
To be washed—
To unfold—
And be told

The meaning of every moment in their lives—
Women who went
In search of God
And sought redemption
In suicide bombs—
Then searched through the shrapnel
Looking for themselves
And their beliefs that were
Cast out there—
Somewhere on the other side.
But oh well!
We are here and they are there.
Somewhere on the other side of our beliefs
Were all these women
Who went down to the well
In search of love
With nervous breakdowns,
Who tried to cry,
But for some reason
The stubborn waters
Just wouldn't fall,
Because somewhere on the other side
Of their dried-up wells of tears
Were their fears,
And their dreams,
And the women
On the other side of who they were—
And had hoped that they would someday be—
Balanced women,
And not barren
Who went down to the well
With empty buckets and became
Unstable as water—
Frozen in time—
Conformed to the limits of their physical universe—
Loosened by the flow they didn't even know
That we would now be flowing in—
As we all vaporize into pure dust and air.

But we are here and they are there
Somewhere on the other side—
And oh well!
Well, is it a deep well, or is it a shallow well?
Is what our mothers always said:
Well I don't know—
Well I think I know—
Well you know—
Well no I don't know—
Well no means no—
Well no sometimes means yes—
Well yes I love you—
Well yes I love you—But
Well but what?
Well what will be will be—
Well be that as it may—
Well maybe—
Well—well—well—well—well—
How deep are the wells that we have been living in?
How deep are the wells that we have been drowning in?
How deep are the wells that we have been dying in?
Well, you don't miss the water
Until the well runs dry
Is what our mothers always said—
But they never told us
Why.

V. A Hole in the Well

And then we are stuck in the well—
In a hole of nothing
Wondering how nothing has a hold on us?
Because nothing in the hole
Likes to make us feel
That there is something in the hole
Worth opening up to—
Worth looking into—
Worth surrendering to—

And in order for us to make it
Out of the hole of nothing,
We have to hold on to nothing.
Now isn't that something?—
No that is nothing!
Because
Something has to be in the water
Because remember that is what our mothers always said—
The same something that has passed
Down our mother's words,
Through Swahili and Greek and Arabic and Sanskrit.
Yes, something is there that connects us to
The mother tongue—
Written down there in the written word
In logographic, syllabic, and alphabetic writings.
For before we could finish learning our *ABCs*,
We all were forced to confront the question
Y?

VI. *The Storybooks of Our Lives*

Why?—Z!
Is what our mothers always said:
And now that you know your ABCs
Next time won't you play with me?
So we play with the *ABCs* of life
And respond to unanswered letters
To write the stories of our lives—
For in the books of our lives
Are the double-helix meanings
Written down in our genetic codes—
In the three billion letters of our chromosomes,
Each letter a chemical building block of
Adenine,
Guanine,
Cystosine,
Thymine.
Yes, something is there that bonds the

As to the *G*s and the *C*s to the *T*s—
The same something that bonds
Our *ABCDEFG*s—
Something that makes
A hole—whole
And the well—well.
Well!
Something has to be in the water—
That is unseen between
The hydrogen and the oxygen bonds
Which are forever transforming
The clouds in the skies—
Where stars fall into each other's arms
Spiraling and clustering into
Galaxies of families—
Yes, something is there
Lying
At the cores of all families—
Darkness.
In the souls of black holes
That house the masses of millions of suns—
The sons of gamma-ray photons which
Interlock with electrons
And spermlike protons—
Descendants of something
Consecrated out there in the cosmic seas
Of high-energy radiation—
Which cause our universe
To become transparent.
For it is apparent
That we are not just scattered objects
Passing through the clouds,
Yet we are often unable to see the
Glory
Of who we are—
Because we are here.
But why?

VII. *Coming Up for Breath*

Why are we here like
Virgins in limbo—
Waiting on someone
To unravel the mysteries of who we are—
Waiting on somewhere to be right here
And not somewhere on the other side—
Waiting on that something that has to be in the water
That is sexual and mystical,
Unavoidably responsible
For the madness between you and I,
So please forgive the madness
But that is who we are—
Virgins in limbo,
Who are lying in waiting,
Wondering—
When will this world come to an end?
For no one knows exactly when and why
Our world will end,
But we can only choose to believe
It will end the same way it began,
Conceived in love,
For there was evening and
There was morning today—
Today
We must wrap our legs
Around the clouds,
Thrust our souls into the
Pelvis of the universe,
And suck the breath
From the breast of Mother Earth.
For somewhere at her core
Are the dreams of our mothers and our grandmothers,
And our own unbeknownst dreams—
Dreams that are buried
At the bottom of the ocean,

Weighed down by a
Tiny strand of sand that bonds with another—
Tiny strand of sand that bonds with another—
Tiny strand of sand that bonds our dreams in bondage,
Yet the water flows.
And so we go with the flow
We don't even know we are flowing in.
But what we do know is that in order for us
To live and to breathe,
We must come up for air,
And it is there—
Right here,
Not somewhere on the other side of these unstable waters
We will breathe our first orgasmic breath.
Hmmmmmmmm!

MY SISTER'S SHOWER SONG

Bathtub bubbles burst
With memories
Of you and me playing together
In blue soap suds of
Life
That wash us away,
Only to lather us in films of dirt
And expose us
In the darkrooms of our memories
Each day.

Today's remembrance
Is when I stole your red rubber ducky.
You were four and I was three.
I still can remember your spongy cries
For I was there. Now.
Today I only hear the echoes of your cries
As they howl in the vortex down the drain.

Today we stand in solitude showers,
Singing songs of
Save me,
Shame,
Sorrow.

Singing songs of regrets
Of how our childhood tomorrows
Didn't reflect
The perfect homes with yellow patios,
Where sun-baked sand pies parched
Beneath the auburn-crusted sunsets
That we rode off to
On the convertible back
Of your one little red rubber ducky.

Growing up means letting go
And holding on
To the memories that we know:
When you were four and I was three,
When we first learned
To wash each other
As we sat with the spirit,
High up on its footstool.
And we were ready,
And we were waiting
To be washed!

MEMORY

it was two o'clock on a wednesday morning
and i went to sleep and i lost
my mind/in my memory's memory
i remember remembering
your boisterous whisper
walking through my
blind/eye/remember
remembering you coming into my
home/coming into my temple/my soul
you walked through
my living room/straight
into the backyard of my mind.
i suppose i was juxtaposed
as i stood/moving
on the threshold of insanity
watching the reality of humanity
walk by me in the morning
of the night/in the morning of the night
i lay there benighted/highlighted.
in my memory's memory
were the regenerated thoughts of
my generation's whispers
whispering/in the morning
of the night.

in my memory's memory
i remember remembering
the hollow/cost
of live bloodless bones of flesh
buried beneath mountains of
memories of bloodless bodies
whispering/in my memory's memory.
i remember remembering
walking on the cross/roads/
of crack sidewalk vials/miles
upon miles.
i remember remembering
gracefully dancing on point
of bloodless needle tip/toeing away.
my mind remembers the
whispering/in my memory's memory.
i remember remembering
showing up late and being thankful i survived
the drive-bys/that rode off
with my family's lives/sitting at an
empty thanksgiving feast
with my ancestors' favorites recipes
passed down through the middle passage
of a bloodless slave/saved mastered
sea/i sat and ate the remnants of
their leftover lamb's bone,
sucked on the marrow,
drowning in sorrow,
not knowing if i could face tomorrow's
whispering/in my memory's memory.
i remember remembering

the/end/of/men/squared/away
in my mind is the bloodless
crushing of the democracy conspiracy
that was imbedded in me
since the beginning of
mankind's time/remembers the
whispering in my memory's memory.
i remember remembering
an old life-filled baby
dangling
on a bloodless ummm/biblical cord
cut off/dropped
into a can of garbage.
the baby was only able to manage
to cry and to breathe
abba/abba/abba/abba/abba/abba/abba/abba/abba/abba.
the baby was
plunging
falling
bawling
whispering/in my memory's memory.
i remember remembering
whispering,
where is god in all of this?
because it was two o'clock
on a wednesday morning,
and i went to sleep,
and i lost my/mind/if i remind you
that my memory does not remember

the exact moment
in the morning of the night when
i went to sleep and lost my
mind's/memory remembers
the exact moment
of the morning of the day
waking up/the exact
infinite moment of
con/temporary insanity/temporary
reality/boisterously whispering,
by whose unauthorized authority
did you come into my
home/come into my temple/my soul,
walk through my living room
and picnic in the backyard of my
mind/knows that when insane it remembers
sane/and sane remembers
pain/and pain remembers
joy/and joy remembers
hope/and hope remembers
fear/and fear remembers
trust/and trust remembers
faith/and faith remembers
real/and real remembers
lies/and lies remember
truth/and truth remembers
death/and death remembers life
whispers,
do you remember the blood?

AIR POCKETS

FAST DRIVER

I want to let the top down
And roll like
Chinese-checker marbles
In and out of
Yellow, green, red, white, and blue lives
On the road,
Knowing all men eventually make it home.
Except that one little black marble
With no one to get over,
Stranded in a hole
And no longer alive to play with toy cars.

LOOSE

Dedicated to my next-door neighbor.
the world knew her as Millicent Eudora Gadsby—
but I called her Lucy Luce.

You have to experience me
As I breaststroke through my
Cheyne-Stoke breath,
Diving in and out of death and life.

Beneath each chasm in my last gasps for breath
Lies the life of every moment I have ever known.

Losing myself,
I am loosened by affliction and affection.

It is then you will know my pain.
It is then you will know my joy.
It is then you will know that I am a woman
Who was meant to be known and
Experienced.

A SIMPLE MOVE

Somewhere
Here inside this space,
There must be a place
For me to move
To another realm of self-expression.

A simple move,
Not removing who I am.

But a simple move
Out of the way.

For me to make a way
To simply
Move.

THE BILL OF BIRTH RIGHTS

Inspired by Luke 17, John 3, Galatians 5, and Hebrews 4

We all have issues—
Issues that sue us in the courtrooms of our minds
And incarcerate our entire beings
In the small cellblocks of our brains.

We all show up to this courtroom
With a small briefcase of
Defendable, unclaimed, identifiable baggage
That weighs us down
To cop pleas
To live in solitary confinement
Instead of living out mandatory
Life sentences.
We all have issues.

Issues that began at birth
When we came out
And took our first glimpse
Of the world
And said, *Oh no.*
So we made a detour,
And we breached ourselves
Between our mother's legs.
But she kept pushing us out
When the water broke
And time said it was time for us to be
Baptized into life.
And she kept pushing us
Out of those greatly increased childbearing pains, screaming:

Come out, come out, wherever you are!
Wherever that place is
We then discovered
Our entire lives
Would be centered around
Playing hide-and-seek from.
And it was at that epiphany
That our first issues began.
But still, she kept pushing us out
And pushing our ashy skins out
To serve as ashtrays for her
Burnt-out cigarettes,
And her burnt-out dreams,
And her burnt-out realities
That a child could not be brought into this world
To fill the void
That has been passed down from
One generation,
To another generation,
To another generation,
To another generation,
Through the long lineage of the
Baby-mama-drama-trauma cycle.
Yes, we all have issues.

One of the biggest issues we have
Is that we find pleasure
In the fact that we have
Fewer issues than others.
We didn't grow up
In the stereotypical
Dysfunctional home:
In a sexually,
Or an emotionally,
Or a physically,
Or a psychologically
Abusive household.
But instead we grew up

In a two-parent home,
In a two-story house,
With two loving siblings attending
Ballet recitals and soccer practices,
With a two-car garage
Housing a Toyota Camry and an SUV
With big-screen TVs,
And satellite dishes
With computer access
That connected us
To disconnect us from
Reality—
That subliminal belief
That we all are somehow
"Normal."
A normal child
Happily going to school
With a lunch box
Filled with tuna fish
Until we arrived and saw
All of the other kids
With peanut butter and jelly sandwiches,
And it was that kind of small moment,
However trivial,
That scarred some of us for life,
And branded others with guilty complexes,
Because we survived from
Developing inferiority complexes,
While their small issues
Went through metamorphosis
And were transformed into the likes
Of eating disorders
That we endorsed by buying their images
On magazine covers
Instead of spending our money to feed kids
With societal-imposed anorexia
In Africa and Sri Lanka
And right here in our own backyards in America.

Yes, I said we all have issues.
Some deep down home-sewn and grown issues!

Issues whose names
Became such big issues they had to be renamed.
We have gone from stupid to dyslexic.
Crazy to schizophrenic.
We are manic-depressive,
Obsessive-compulsive,
Anal-retentive,
Plagued with every phobia
And social anxiety and seasonal affective disorders.
And yes, some of us feel
This is all psychological mumble jumble—
But hey, that is your own personal issue.
And why do we always feel the need
To make our personal issues somebody else's issues?

We admire issues that are
Decked out and dressed
In the biggest issue,
Stress.
We are stressed out about being
Too short,
Too tall,
Too fat,
Too small.
Our breasts are too big,
Our breasts are too small.
We are too dark,
Too light,
Too smart,
And too dumb.
We numb the stress
By becoming drug addicts,
Alcoholics,
Pedophiles,
And convicts.

We have major issues with life
Because it seems that we are always a paycheck away
From being homeless, that we ignore,
Like defenseless
Children on the brink of extinction,
Who can't understand why the wildlife
Is more important than their very own lives.

Our hair is too curly,
Too kinky,
Too thin.
Our lives revolve around bad hair days so
That we don't even have the time to consider the woman
Who lost her hair to chemotherapy,
Because we spend half of our lives in therapy,
Which just lets us know
What we already know,
That we all have issues!

We are so obsessed with ourselves
We can walk out on our husbands and our children,
But we can't leave home without our cells,
Hungry and lonely as we watch
Our fathers kill our mothers and themselves
In front of our very own eyes.
We've got fake eyes,
And fake hair,
And fake lives,
And we constantly deny
Denial that we all have issues.
We always believe we are
Keeping it real,
So we just keep giving it up
Without knowing what
It is.
Because what it is,

Is
That we all have issues.

And the real issue is often between
You and God.
Because He is the one
Who brought you into the world,
And He is the one
Who is going to take you out.

So come out,
Come out,
Wherever you are
Because that kingdom of God
Is neither here nor there,
But the kingdom of God is within you.
And just imagine how many issues we must have
Because most of our lives we can't see that?
Issues that began at birth
When the water broke
And Time said it was time to be baptized into life.
When we came out
And took our first glimpse at the world and said
Oh no
Instead of oh yes
Because living with issues
Primarily is only a matter of perspective.

"And now surely we cannot enter a second time
Into our mother's womb
To be born again,
But I tell you the truth,
In order to enter into the kingdom of God,
We must go within,
The water must break,
And we must be born of Spirit
Because the fruit of the Spirit is love,
And the fruit of the Spirit is joy,

And the fruit of the Spirit is peace,
And the fruit of the Spirit is patience
And kindness
And goodness
And faithfulness
And gentleness,
And the fruit of the Spirit is self-control.
And against such things there is no law"
That can unshackle and set us free from these issues
Which sue us in the courtrooms of our minds
And incarcerate our entire beings in the small
Cellblocks of our brains.
We all show up to this courtroom with a small briefcase of
Defendable, unclaimed, identifiable baggage
That weights us down.
Yes, we all have issues!

But I have the issue
Of living behind these
Pretentious defensive mechanisms
Which are based on the false premises
That I will be acquitted
Because the burden of proof
Rests in the verdict
Of how do I forgive God
Who knew I was going to grow up
With parents who painted me black and blue,
Who knew the color of my skin
Would cast me out on the periphery
Or cause people to assume that I was born a racist.
And how do I forgive God
Who gave me the freedom to hate?
The freedom to love?
The freedom to rape?
The freedom to prefer the color red over blue?
Or choose eggplants over mushrooms?

Or choose to abort a child
Or love a child
Without a cry
Stillborn to forgive?
How do I forgive God for this gift of freedom?
Because I don't just want to be free,
But I want to be free indeed.

Because freedom indeed
Is not a deed bound in a creed
On a piece of paper
Or passed down through judicial legislature
And ratified in the Bill of Rights
And constitutional amendments
Which were designed
To free and enslave people both at the same time,
With the freedom of religion, speech, and press
And the right of assembly
And the right to bear arms.
But freedom indeed comes
When I am walking in the Spirit
Which isn't defined or confined by man-made laws
Or concerned with search and arrest and civil procedures.

For when the Spirit comes,
It searches the hearts and examines the mind,
"It is sharper than any double-edged sword,
It penetrates even to dividing soul and spirit,
Joints and marrow;
It judges the thoughts and attitudes of the heart."
And when my heart stops,
I can't seek
I can't find
That this life is not a game.
I can't run
I can't hide

Behind myself
And plead the fifth.

So come out,
Come out,
Wherever you are
With your hands up in the air
And wave a white flag like you just don't care.
And if you know that you have an issue,
Then say, *Oh yeah!*
Because we all have issues!